I0146762

Man In My Shoes
My Cross-Dressing Husband

By
Brianna Doylan

Hidden Shoe Press

ISBN 978-1-906921-01-9

Copyright © 2022 by Brianna Doylan
All rights reserved by Hidden Shoe Press. No part of this book may be reproduced in any manner whatsoever without written permission except in the case of brief quotations embodied in critical articles and reviews.
First Printing, 2022

Cover image purchased under licence from iStock.

TABLE of CONTENTS

FOREWORD 5

The Mirror 6
My Story, Her Story, Our Story 7
Knowing 8
The Lady 10
Why Tell Me At All 13
The New Normal 14
Show Me 16
Funeral Pyre 18
What Next 20
Perspective 21
It Started Long Ago 22
Back To My Story 24
One Rule For Her 25
Only Clothes 28
Truce 29
Competition 30
And The World Keeps Turning 32
Stolen 34
Just A Normal Day 35
Aftermath 36
Moving Forward Forever 39
City Life 44
400 Square Feet 45
400 Square Feet 2 47
And Again 49
Home Again 53
I Don't Know Why 58
Facing The Nemesis 60
Boundaries Of Revelation 68
The Mirror Reprise 69
What happened to Brianna? 70

3

Foreword

Brianna never set out to be a cross-dresser's Wife, but as is often the case, this is what she became.

If you are looking for an insight into cross-dressing, a heartfelt and empathic account of one couples' story, then this could be your path. Follow Brianna's ever-changing life in this fascinating underworld, where acceptance seems to belong, in fact, to no genre at all.

From stark revelation, through the pain and difficulty of exploring why this shift in genre can be so difficult, Brianna gives an honest and heartrending account of how she and her Husband coped with the elusive boundaries of things which simply cannot be changed.

You may be shocked or amazed at how, or indeed why, this couple survived the surprises. Follow their journey of solidarity in an everyday world which knew nothing of their personal situation.

Humour runs through the narrative as you meet colourful characters along the way. But you will also find sadness for an existence which for many, has little help or support.

Brianna takes you through several decades of her life and draws you into her world of confusion and indecision. This leads her to a positive route of self-discovery and understanding, which sometimes brings unexpected triumph.

If this is also your story and you, too, are travelling this path, there is no right or wrong; Your conclusion will be yours and yours alone.

This is Brianna's adventure.
Did she stay? Or did she leave?

Read on...........

The Mirror

What do you see
When you look in the mirror?
    Who stares back at you
    And what do you feel?

        What do you think that
        Your image compares with?
            Do you believe that
            This woman is real?

Is there a day when
She doesn't exist for you?
    How will she age
    As your life passes by?

        Why is it her who's your
        Number one lady?
            Can you not see that
            The mirror can lie?

MY STORY - OUR STORY - HER STORY

And so, it began........

It was hard to know why this was the chosen moment, though we later agreed that the initial shock could have been better delivered in more subtle terms.

"There's something I have to tell you," he said, with an air of matter of fact, tinged with devastation.

With the innocence of the naive, he pulled no punches

"I'm a transvestite"

"Sorry, Transvestite's a bit strong – it's Cross-dressing these days."

It was done from a standing start, full of bravado, where the Lady skidded to a halt, metaphorically, in the middle of my bedroom, taking no heed of any red lights along the way.

As the bottom started to dissolve from my world, I could never have imagined what lay before me, in all its' complexity. This one secret protected yet affected so many.

She did her best.

"I don't do it much, nothing really, mostly just tights under my trousers. I don't want to go out like it."

"Oh, yes. And shoes." (Looks guilty). "I do love stiletto heeled shoes. I'm not gay," (panic in voice), "honest. I'm just a normal bloke who fancies women."

"I, I..... love you - you won't leave me, will you?"

I shook my head, slowly, having no idea of how else to react.

The hope in her eyes lit the room.
In my mind, she rose on imaginary stilettos and sashayed well and truly into my life, stripping away the first layers of my own identity and wellbeing.

<u>Knowing</u>

There are things which cannot be unseen or forgotten.

There are many wonderful people out there who can know things, accepting of the situation, no matter how much it hurts.
People who manage not to comment, judge, or ask questions.

I am not one of those people.
I found myself being analytical, seemingly realistic and ultimately self-destroying in my need to know.

My mind could not rest.

I had lived through many things and my instinct was to cope.
It is what we naturally do – problems need solutions, illness needs treatment and life, naturally needs compromise.
Simple, if said quickly.

I was to learn much.
It's not all bad and there are good moments to come.
But those who know will appreciate that my story is lifelong, despite the initial "quick fix" attitude to just get on with life.

Of course, life was, indeed, never the same again.
It never will be.

There is much to be gained through understanding of a problem, although this particular problem uncovers the realisation that you cannot treat a non-illness and you will need to tackle things in life where compromise will ultimately be unequal.

There is much fact and so much more in theory about cross-dressing. Most importantly, there is essential soul searching and too much emotion.

Ironically, would I have stayed at all if it wasn't for the unseen bond to the Lady? I believe that the answer, surprisingly, would be NO.

I stayed because of an extra level of loyalty and protection.

Her need.
But ultimately, LOVE.

8

My mind set off on a racing and ever changing tangent, from which it would never fully recover. I sat in silence, trying to take it all in, with emotions becoming increasingly vivid.

I felt an incredible sense of loss, mourning.

Initially it felt like being dumped for someone else, when the empty feeling kicks in and you realise that you are losing all you hold dear and wondering what comes next. Except, of course, that in this case, it felt like my husband was "leaving" me in the normal sense, but replacing what I had with his pseudo identity, which mirrored, as is often the case, me, his Wife.

It felt like my husband was being replaced by another woman. I began to wonder what on earth any acceptance meant for me. Was I now supposed to be attracted to women?

The colours increased and the vivid picture accelerated.

My mind was spinning, but I wasn't seeing a flamboyant drag queen. Tights had instantly taken on a new level of importance and the thought of the sweaty, itchy feeling of hidden gusset under clothing made me feel quite strange. I was imagining every man in the world just "keeping warm" in tights and omg, how many of them really got off on it?

Trying to rationalize, I bravely cracked a one liner that at least the mediocre level of "just tights" did not seem too big a deal. I would soon learn to beware of opening the doors to Her opportunities.

"So, would you mind if I wore tights under my trousers some days?" She said, "And if it's not asking too much, occasionally some high heeled shoes?"

"Casually, while we're watching telly?" I replied, with a sarcastic edge, secretly wondering what the hell this situation meant for me.

"That would be nice. I'm just trying to be honest, no more lies."

"Just a "normal" evening then," I whispered, "No going back now."

And off we went.

The Lady

So, let's meet the actual Lady.

From the beginning, or should I say, from my beginning. The start of my relationship with the Nemesis who is also my Husband.

Zabina is a very pretty name.
In protecting her true identity, I choose to call my Husband Zabina.

On this particular occasion, I am the one who gets to choose. My actions are fictitious because I change the name of a Lady who does not exist.
Except that she does.

Zabina is my cross-dressing husband.
And she can never leave.

To start with, like most, I knew absolutely nothing about cross-dressing and even less about cross-dressers.

In my naivety, I had always considered, wrongly, that transvestites, or cross-dressers, were mainly Drag Queens.

My reaction to a man in women's clothes was one of fascination, admiration for their courage and perhaps a little bit of distaste.

One day, in a high street, someone shouted "there's a man over there dressed in ladies' clothes!" I was as quick as anyone else to rush over to see just what the man in question was wearing and how he looked!

Quite simply, if someone who isn't in your life is dressing in ladies' clothes, it is fascinating and interesting.

When your own partner is the cross-dresser, it is very different.

It is only then that you understand how often the subject crops up in general conversation and how you find yourself lying about what you know. Laughing with others at the decidedly not so funny.

You learn to live your life by hiding, where you cannot reveal a topic which is a little too strange for shared discussion in company.

10

My initiation into the world of my new Husband was not as smooth as Her ideal vision of belonging in mine.

In fairness, the transition she had dreamed of was less than well-oiled and it is no wonder that many crash at the first hurdle without even raising an elegant heel to clear the bar.

He was very well prepared.

Even now, many, many years since my story began, the world of cross-dressing is, perhaps, the hardest to comprehend.
We have come a long way towards acceptance of different gender identity and the world is a good place if you can find out who you are and can identify with your comfortable space in the world.

Herein lies the difference in the life of the average cross-dresser.

Simply put, to be gay is to enjoy people of your own sex. To be transexual is a desire to become and belong to the opposite sex. To be non-binary is to be non-specific to either gender. And so on...

Cross-dressers identify mainly within their original sex. As the clothes and temporary persona cross into the opposite gender, a cross-dressing man generally has no wish to be or become female.

People also make the mistake that cross-dressing relationships fit into the neat box of transvestite men and straight women. Not so.

The Drag Queen empire is often labelled as flamboyant and "camp," but people from all genders can be cross-dressers.

I have had more than one gay friend crying in my arms when a partner wanted to dress as their "opposite." With little acceptance or understanding, in this example, a gay man, falling in love with a gay man, had no more desire for a pseudo woman than I did.

And so on, wherever you may belong, there will always be those who cross-dress towards the "other side."

I never imagined how many "sub-genders" existed in groups of people who were mostly happy with their original sex.

And how the groups rarely coincide, because "I'm not like THEM."

Returning to Zabina, the thing she endorsed most was always "I'm just a normal bloke who fancies women."
This is not an easy thing to absorb.

As my stomach sank, with the feeling that none of this news was good, I tried to rationalize to stay sane.

So my husband was a cross-dresser, who was a normal bloke who fancied women; he didn't want to be a woman, merely to look like one. Excuse me if I was a little overcome.

We talked.
The compulsion, the need, the desire to "dress," the feel of silky fabric. And of course, the shoes.

I distinctly remember thinking aloud as the red started to rise at this perception of "normal."

Zabina defended her corner in a strange mixture of sulky teenage rebellion and articulate, all controlling madam.

The words spilled out of my mouth, despite the knowledge that I would be shot down in flames.

"I thought you were going to tell me about an affair, but I never imagined that the other woman would be you.
I honestly wish you had told me you were gay; At least then you would know what you are. It would have been easier."

"I'm – not - GAY, I'm a normal bloke, I don't fancy MEN."

"I understand that you don't fancy men" I retorted, "So what makes you think that I'm going to fancy a WOMAN?"

Once the words started to emerge, I could not help myself.
"And if I was going to sleep with a woman, I'd prefer a real one if you don't mind, at least they know what a real woman wants."

Silence cut through the air.
Zabina is the way she is. She does not always want to be this way.

But she is.
Knowing the compulsion, that she cannot help it, does not help me.

12

Why Tell Me At All?

I think I omitted to tell you that the secret was revealed when I was at my happiest? At the end of a perfect day, whilst sipping a late nightcap, during a long awaited holiday.

Never again in my life would I comment about happiness without thinking, "Be careful, don't get confident." Because dreams are prone to being shattered.

I often question why I needed to know about Zabina at all.

But there was always going to be part of this strange, female entity which wanted to reveal herself to the world. Part of the hard to maintain disguise that all is normal. It had to start by coming clean.

She needed honesty, at least with me, before she could attempt resolution of exactly whom she wanted to be.

And guilt. Always, always, guilt. Because we carry more burdens over the things which are inevitable. The things for which we have no control. And the things we cannot avoid.

Fortunately, the modern world is much more tolerant of need, desire and preference and there is easier access to professional help regarding self-awareness, choice and consequence.

But what of the wives and partners?

Cross-dressing is not the sort of confidence that you can betray to the world when you need to talk. A man wearing women's clothes is hardly a criminal offence. And there are, indeed, those who enjoy the experience together.

But most cross-dressers stay firmly behind closed doors. Less of a hidden "agenda" as a "hiding gender."
So, it's hard to admit why you aren't performing well at work, can't cope with life, or why you don't confide in your friends or family.

Cross-dressing is often a lonely place. But just knowing can be desolate, as the partner remains silent.

Anyway, best be quiet. For what would the world think of me?

The New Normal

Watching TV was not a great success.

She appeared, bashful and timid, heels clicking across the parquet. "Thank you for this. Are you sure you don't mind? I do love you."

I said nothing as I drank in the vision, feeling that a gentle stroll had suddenly turned into a roller-coaster.

It seemed that the requirements had moved on a little.
The tights and shoes "felt as if they looked stupid" under tracksuit bottoms, so She wore a rather nasty little denim mini skirt.

The red mist acknowledged this; "You don't say."

As tights and shoes looked "strange" with a man's t-shirt, a tight, glittery little teenage top had emerged, accompanied by some tissues stuffed hurriedly into a badly fitting bra.

The clash of tarty colours annoyed me.
And the smell of unwashed clothes, repeatedly stuffed hurriedly out of sight, made me feel more than a little sad.

It did not feel right.
It didn't look right either.

I had quickly done some research into the subject and began to appreciate that lone cross-dressing has no peer support to apply the brakes. Therefore, it came as no great surprise that "most girls needed help" was a phrase of the understatement.

Grateful that we had more than one seat and I didn't have to share, I declined the offer of a cuddle. She understood, "I don't blame you to be honest, not with me looking like this. I wouldn't either."

We settled down to watch a film and drank some wine. Observing carefully, I could not deny that Zabina looked happy.

"It helps me to relax," she purred contentedly.

I was not relaxed. "Glad he's just a normal bloke," I thought drily to myself. "Still, could be worse. No wig or bright blue eyeshadow."

And so, the new normal began, if normal is how we continued. I will not deny the difficulties from both sides.

On the first day back at work, I watched my husband dress in his usual undergarments and lower layers. Then, Zabina seductively pulled on tights, smoothing them, being careful not to snag, unintentionally glancing shyly in the mirror. Finally, quickly, the trousers and expected top layers were added, the working boots of the job in hand. The start of his normal day.

My heart pounded as I absorbed these actions with an inward shudder; I had just witnessed two different people carrying out the simple process of getting ready for work. Together.

Instinctively, I at last understood that not all men who wore tights to keep warm would worship the garment in this way. My husband was, without any shadow of a doubt, a real-life cross-dresser.

As I tried to adjust to the uninvited stranger, my husband was affected by the guilt of my burden, but more so from the guilt of Her enjoyment in being set free.

On Her good days, Zabina positively bathed in a glow I had never seen before.

I can't recall my own good days. But it wasn't all bad.

I created a relationship with Zabina, which quickly became protective of this fragile, inner being; a child growing in confidence, always testing the boundaries, disputing any limitations and ultimately challenging any reprisal.

But now it was me who held onto the secret.

The days turned into weeks. Normality of day-to-day life and social interaction resumed, as I was swept along with the flow. Zabina wasn't around every day, which felt like a reprieve. Until the next time, when the absence made Her return seem even more powerful.

My husband was so caring; indebted for all that I did, all that I was.

In a former life, I would have felt admired, flattered. But in feeling emotionally numb, I was unaware that the red mist was rising.

15

Show me

I tried so hard to let it all go, to be at peace, to relax. After all, this was still my Husband and outwardly, life had not changed.

But I could not let it go.
Like a dog with a bone, I had to keep digging. "What do you want Zabina to be? What's she like?"

Zabina, so I was told, was a wannabe party girl and, as chosen by many, she favoured the style of stilettos, short skirts and blonde wigs. In my younger days, in fact when I met my husband, so did I. It was probably what caused the fatal attraction. Except, may I add, for the wig. I have never felt the need for a wig.

During one of our long and frequent talks, which I knew were going round and round in the same circle, I kept asking why. Each time he explained, the boundaries became extended to include more needs, more wants, just one more thing. Until, of course, the next time.

Maybe I pushed towards the worst scenario to get it over with. There is nothing worse than being drip fed a story, knowing the finale, but hoping that it would stop here, with no more to find out, no more to know.

But this was for real.
There is no "cure." No-one can really explain why normal men have this desire. And the truth is that in an ideal world, the dream is to dress as a woman, go out into the world and "pass;" that is, to be believable as a woman in public. Then return home to the Wife.

This was real.
Although Zabina knew it was unlikely to happen, "how nice it would be if we both dressed the same (the whole lot, stockings, short skirts and of course, stiletto heeled shoes) and had sex."

This was very real.
I felt as if the life was being sucked from my being, leaving me bewildered by this hypnotic creature, like an unending gothic tale. My captor's clothing was red. Bright, bright red.

"Show Me," I said.
"Show Me"

16

And so, she did.
The real Zabina, who hadn't a clue.

My Husband didn't want to let go, to let me see all there was, to leave himself bare for ridicule. But he did it.

Tiny red panties, black stockings, would-be-white suspenders. Black bra, tiny leather skirt, pink blouse. Not quite stilettos. "All they had in my size," She said, "there isn't a lot of choice in charity shops." There was an anguish in her eyes, a longing for better.

She stopped short of makeup and wig. Though did comment that it "obviously looked better when you did it properly."
Properly.
I felt incredibly sad as this melancholy creature touched every nerve in my body and crawled deep into my soul.

That was it.
Zabina stood around for a few moments, looking very uneasy, before desperately needing to get away. She took off the bargain bucket rags and stuffed them back into a stripey carrier bag.
And She was gone.

It took a few glasses, but I slept.
I had seen the worst it was to be for me and now I knew.
Truly, I had no idea how to feel, but the ice in my heart melted with love and sympathy for this creature with nowhere to belong.

But morning came and the seesaw changed; tipped its balance.
Panic rising in my mind; "How can I do this; Why should I do this?"

Anger rising up inside; Red, red mist.
"Why me? Why did you pick on me. You must have known?"

"I thought I was cured. You cured me; I didn't want to do it again, not after I was with you. But it came back; I couldn't help it. Sorry."

"Sorry? SORRY?!"
The red mist took over. I grabbed the stripey carrier bag, running down the stairs, out of the house and into the garden.
On the path, I set light to the contents of the bag. I set light to Her.

He stood in the garden, watching. Only then, did I see the tears.

17

Funeral Pyre

In my mind she stood
Like a cheap caricature of City Chic

Red

I saw red and flashing anger
With bright lights whirling through my mind
Hating you
But hating Her most of all

Run, I run through the house
Grabbing the tarty glitter
And back to the garden

There
There on the garden path
With the neighbours thinking me mad
I burned the clothes
And I burned Her

But I burned Him too
As remains melted onto the path
One half-surviving stiletto
Like a curling semi-cremated character
From a B movie

With eyes full of defeat and loss
But most of all
Mourning
Only then did I see the tears

I had destroyed Her

Oh, how He was hurting
And so was I
As with silent dignity
He still needed me

And I knew I loved him

But next day
She was back in the bargain bins

An opportunity

After all
All girls love shopping
For new clothes

What Next

I wasn't proud of my actions, but in the words of Zabina, "I couldn't help it." I now understood more about my Nemesis, for the compulsion had been so strong; unavoidable; I simply had to do it.

My Husband said very little. I think I may have felt better if he had berated me, shouted, screamed in the vicious tongue of his female counterpart. But this was not the man I knew at all. My Husband was feisty, sometimes arrogant and often dismissive of my angst. This silence unnerved me; I didn't know what to do.

Naturally, I apologised.
He laid no blame at my door, taking full responsibility.
I was mortified, brimming with guilt about the amount of distress I had caused. This new outlook made me realise just how fragile I had become; how ironically, guilt was the thing that mortified me.

My whole world was fragile. In just one moment, our whole world had fallen apart and I had no direction, no path. No guidance.

We sat, staring at the embers on the path, as if it happened like this every Sunday morning. The cremated heel had finally stopped squirming and we sat quietly in the sun.

"We can't go on like this," I said at last. "I can't go on like this."
"Few people can," he answered, calmly. "I don't expect you to stay with someone like me, I do understand."

"I'm not sure I do," I continued. "I don't want to lose you, lose us; but I don't know if I can live with Her. I need time."

The sun was getting warmer and nothing happened for a while, as if time had stood still. I was transfixed by the half living stiletto, it's unmarked tip still ready for the click, click of a willing Lady on a shiny, wooden floor. Or maybe marble. Click, click, clickety click.

"I'll clear this mess up," he said.
Zabina placed the revered and charred remains gently in the stripey carrier bag, eyes full of unshed tears. I never saw the items again.

"Bit early for a drink," came the icebreaker.
"Coffee first then?" he replied.

20

Perspective

Before I send my readers running for the hills, I think I should take a break from events and try to explain how it feels to be in this parallel universe of a cross-dressers Wife.

As I mentioned before, it wasn't all bad.
Between the lows of finding out, feeling helpless about what cannot be changed and the minefield of where this left my own identity as a woman, there were good times.

The delicate male, female balance of yours, mine, ours, "you don't understand because you're not like me," took on a new level.
Not only did I have this Nemesis full of jealousy and conflict, but I now had a confidante in all things female, someone to talk to about this unexpected turn of events.

My new best friend and ally against a world that knew nothing.

Likened by some to an affair, Zabina was not an affair.
Those who would suggest divorce should see that this marriage had not broken down; I had not fallen out of love with my Husband.

In times ahead, between the hurt, rage and red mist, came much soul searching, talking and the inevitable tears of both sadness and understanding. I learnt to appreciate a new and different kind of love with this undeniably strange and at times, pathetic creature.

You may read this in disbelief and feel that it does not exist, cannot exist. You probably wonder why or how I stayed, thinking that I must have lost my mind.
Indeed, what must you think of Women like me?
What does this make Women like me?

It is much more common than you may think.

Take heart if this is also your story.
You will be taken to places where you never intended to go, places which may make or break you in equal measure; and be sure that the Lady will never go away.

But if you feel, at times, that you are losing your mind, trust me, you probably won't.

It Started Long Ago

So how did this rebirth happen, how did Zabina come to be?
Did she just click Her heels on a given day, entering into my
Husband's life with Her shiny stilettos? Did She simply ask to stay?

As I'm sure you can guess, I think not.

Zabina presented Herself, as happens to most people who are this
way, as a gradual feeling of "knowing" and some experimentation.
Instinctively, there was secrecy and shock; fear of being found out.

In Zabina's case, She was young, but not as young as some.
At an age where most young men push boundaries, perhaps my
Husband wore tighter clothes than most of his time, brighter
colours, skimpier summer shorts and had hair that was fashionably,
(though perhaps not this fashionably), long.

If you know the secret, old photographs betray the signs, the love
shown to the camera, the flirtatious, skittish way of this bashful
young creature. Indeed, it is said that the camera never lies.

As the story goes, my Husband had a girlfriend who encouraged
him to "dress." Ironically, before he intended to do so. She adorned
him, as a child dresses a doll, taking him to a party where he would
"enjoy himself." As it turned out, this was not the case. My Husband
felt uncomfortable, self-conscious and confused.

Though he did not enjoy it, his girlfriend did and encouraged him to
go there again. In his own words it "put me off." It would seem that
an invite was not as gratifying as becoming a rebel for the cause.

My Husband did, later and of his own accord, take the path of a
normal man who sometimes liked to dress as a woman. This
eventually heightened to a degree beyond "dressing up," for there
was no denying the acute admiration displayed as Zabina's
reflection was absorbed, greedily, through Her image in the mirror.

Those who have stood at this sexual intersection may find that the
barriers between male and female become blurred and there is, in
fact, no perception, no hint of the Man in the mirror.

Because mirrors often lie.

Over the course of my Husband's normal life, I was interested to know if others had been allowed to share in the unknown?

Allegedly not, although there had, as was explained, been a few social misdemeanours in his younger days, usually involving alcohol, whereby yes, a few people probably "knew" of the fledgling Zabina.

Of course, nothing was ever said. Every established acquaintance I ever met within our social circle was a potential confidante, but no-one, including me, ever gave anything away. The wall of silence, protection, created by us all, was totally stifling.

It was at this point that I felt the resentment rise, the jealousy. When I knew how lonely I was to become.

Why did everyone protect my Husband and Zabina? What was so special about them? And as everyone protected them, I was vulnerable and bare to the wolves of the world.

I remember only one incident in which the star-crossed pair were betrayed. My true understanding would come much, much later.

In the early days of my relationship with my Husband, his ex-girlfriend, a mutual friend, was looking upstairs as he climbed the steps. Wearing summer shorts, in the fashion of the time, he had enviably tanned legs.

"Nice legs," she called, "GIRLS legs!." My husband was unexpectedly abusive, but my friend and I just laughed at his reaction. It felt good to share some humour.

Only after my Husband revealed all, did I appreciate her meaning.

She had known nothing, suspected none of it.
Until, on a whim, she decided to clean the top of a cupboard.

The suitcase fell down, its contents raining down onto the kitchen floor. One stilettoed shoe fell clear of the heap, clattering across the tiles and skidding to a halt in the middle of the cat litter tray.

"The litter tray felt fitting," she said, years after I, myself, had eventually met Zabina. "I do admire you. I couldn't have handled things like you did, I couldn't have stayed with, with …. THAT."

Back To My Story

Returning to the sunny garden, we skipped the coffee in favour of something stronger.

Somehow, life had to go on. It had to continue as close to normal as this new normal could be.

In the days and months which followed the burning, I remember and forget in equal measure, depending on the day. I carried on and no-one, absolutely no-one, learned the secret.

My understanding grew, alongside the feelings that came with living with Zabina. But it's difficult living alongside a man who has no wish to be a woman, but who wants to look so much like a woman that he no longer resembles a man.

Meanwhile, I was a woman who wanted to be a woman who lives with a man who wants to be a man.
And before my Husband intervenes – a man who looks like a man.

I became obsessed with Zabina.

Inwardly, every waking moment was lived within Her world; when I wasn't making compromises for Her existence, I was hating Her with unrivalled venom.

When I wasn't protecting, making concessions for Her every need, we were in combat over Her highly strung demands and I was forever planning Her demise, my escape.

I needed Her out of my life. But I could neither hate nor leave Her compliant host; he who was still my Husband.

Watching him dress reverently in tights was often the trigger, the red tip of the match which again ignited my wrath. Again and again, I demanded answers as to why, if it were so normal, was it such a closely guarded secret. And time and time again I was rewarded with the same answers; that he simply didn't know.

I was pleased if, as my Nemesis, my Husband was happy, relaxed.

But I never watched TV with Zabina again.

One Rule For Her

The simple truth is that if you are to survive, both separately and together, this thing which dominates your life cannot be allowed to dictate every waking moment. At least, not quite.

I learned to partition the emotion. My Husband accepted that mostly, I could function normally. But if the red mist descended, he needed to let me fly as high as was necessary to dispel the rage, the hurt; to let out the frustration and hostility that comes from enforced silence.

Yes, he wore the tights under his trousers, but "only when She felt like it," for which I am grateful, was not every day. I tried to be elsewhere when he got dressed. And my Husband was respectful about how much of Zabina passed through my day.

We learned to interweave our normal existence with a low key Zabina, realising that it was too soon to set Her free into our lives, if ever we could. With little thought for the future, the three of us lived each day as it happened, sharing the battle scars like warriors in a hidden crusade.

But we didn't share it all.

In a relationship where the odds are often two to one against and in my case, I was the underdog, my Husband and Zabina tended to get the lion's share of any rewards, including the compassion.

Evidently, there are things which cannot easily be shared.
We tried to share Zabina and I accepted what existed, no matter how unbelievable or unpalatable; things which according to all accounts and medical research, could never be changed.

We also tried to share my difficulties, why I found it hard to accept that my Husband was "just a normal bloke who….." We have been there before and I will not repeat.

But when there is no actual solution to ease the burden, when one half of the story just "cannot" stop and the other half tries to be all accepting, simply to stay sane, there are bound to be complications.

And I did not feel sane, balanced, or of healthy mind.

It goes without saying that I cannot speak from my Husband's mindset within his psyche. I can only interpret that within his rationalization of self-presence, there was a line which wore an opaque nature, with an impenetrable quality that made it impossible for him to see a normal that was "not quite normal."

Of all the things I witnessed, of all the things I have read and absorbed, to this very day, the concept that blinds me most (and most others who explore this path) is the inability of the cross-dresser to see or accept the mind-blowing impact of this strange, hybrid gender on one's partner.

I am not stupid and as time went on I became less naive. I understood the facts, how harmless all of this must seem to the innocent bystander and the permanence of the situation. I knew that I was the one with the choice to walk away. The luckier one.

That aside, I was getting nothing back where it was most needed. Today, there would be easier avenues to discuss severe mental health issues, but way back then, I felt very much on my own.

I would roam the house when my Husband was out, resisting the maniacal urge to seek Zabina out from her closet and get rid of her arrogance and selfishness, along with everything that She still is.

I would work myself into a frenzy, my stress levels becoming dangerous to both myself and all those around me. I flew into rages as soon as my Husband stepped through the door.

But this type of behaviour would get us nowhere. Been there, done that; time for a new tactic. Albeit a shocking one.

For the first time, I made a liberating decision.
Some would say a first step on the road to recovery.
There are others who would say it was the first step to betrayal.

Because for the first time, I did not choose my Husband.
Neither did I choose Him and Zabina.

Bottom line.
It was a choice between Him and Me.

And I chose Me.

It took a bit of research, a little practice. Admittedly, it was easier from my side of the table. In fact, it didn't feel massively strange at all. Until the last bit.

The final fragment of the transformation.

My Husband came home from work as normal. I made coffee, as usual and as I did so he went upstairs to get changed. I knew that this meant it had been a tights day. He would have had coffee first if it was a non-tights shift. He had no idea that I knew of this habit.

We settled in for the evening. A pleasant evening, a glass of wine with dinner. Watched TV. Just the two of us. Me and my Husband.

I left him to watch a film he had chosen and went quietly from the room to "get my work clothes ready for tomorrow." He sat happily on the sofa and poured more wine. He would need it.

I dressed carefully.
Boxer shorts, chinos, baggy t-shirt with tight boob tube underneath to hold in the bumps. Flat boots.
Hair scraped back and tied away. Thought to self "hell, those wigs must be hot."
And finally, two socks and a roll-on deodorant.

I looked ridiculous. Safe to say I felt ridiculous.

And so, I entered the room. Fast. No time to observe my approach.

I swaggered in like a caricature of a drunken sailor and sat down on the sofa, making sure that I left no room for breathing space between this male-like entity and my Husband.

I have never seen him move so fast. I didn't say a word.
The horror in his eyes was extreme.

He could not get away quick enough, the wine glass overturning on a floor more used to the clickety clack of shiny stilettos.

"Now, do you understand?" I asked, quietly. "Do you still think that it's about nothing more than the clothes you wear?"

"Yes," came the whispered reply. "I understand totally."

Only Clothes

So much more than clothes
Sensations; Padded bits, makeup
Wanting to pass

In any choice of clothing
I do not look like a man
Try to be a man

Until.............
Baggy, shapeless sweatshirt
Flat boots, Chinos
Hair slicked back..........
     And a hard stick of deodorant
      Padded out with a couple of socks

In I swaggered

Your physical revulsion at this male entity
Almost put you into the wall
Behind the sofa
Where you sat

You couldn't get away quick enough

Was this really different
From the things you do?

For surely, it was only clothes
That made the man?

Truce

After this incident, to be fair, things calmed down a little.

We now had comparisons, things to laugh about, such as how ridiculous I looked with socks down my trousers and how daft my Husband felt in work-boots and tights.

Ridiculous, daft.

Those words are, indeed, how things felt on a good day.

Maybe, yes maybe, even that old chestnut, harmless.

In general, regardless of anything else, our friendship had improved and we were allies in the subterfuge of our daily lives. Our relationship became further cemented with the need to protect and support each other, because quite simply, no matter how bad things were between us at any given time, each other was all we had.

Other things, naturally, suffered.

I found it difficult to be physically near my Husband at all. I could not take away the things I had seen and could only imagine the things still to come. I was convinced that this would happen, mostly with the calm certainty of any research I could find, but sometimes with a fear that was untold and unsurmountable. For I was terrified of facing the complete transformation.

In the same way that the socks and deodorant housed in my trousers had made me walk very differently and having seen what the stilettos did to my Husband's gait, I knew instinctively that the wig would be the final metamorphosis, the portal to the complete and unabridged Zabina.

We created a wavelength of acceptance, between the notion of my Husband's desires and the behaviours which I could bear to tolerate. This was the comfort zone, the laughter room, where we were both at ease and found that both of us could speak openly.

We had to start somewhere and it would seem that we had found a beginning, a way to deal with the steady evolution into the parallel universe which housed Zabina, nesting in her lair.

29

Competition

I should explain that it wasn't the frequency of the dressing which caused most damage. It wasn't even the dressing itself. It was the chain of events which followed, the effect it had on both of us and our daily lives.

I appreciated that my Husband was wracked with guilt, ashamed of how he felt about both himself and the things he needed. He showed boundless sorrow regarding how this affected me and how it was destroying our long standing relationship.

But I was still incensed with jealousy, rage and hurt. Occasionally, I was in denial, hoping that I would wake up from the nightmare and find a normal day. But mostly, I was haunted by the knowledge that I needed to be forever silent.

Not that I wanted to rush out and shout from the rooftops, betraying the man I loved. But I was desperately in need of an ally, a confidante. I longed for an independent person who could look beyond emotion and see the situation for what it was. For my despair was like ivy, weaving its twisted vines around my heart.

I even longed for the freedom to chat innocently to a stranger on the bus, without feeling that if I did, I would shock their world. It's not really a conversation starter to say "Hello, how's your morning? I'm going through hell today because I just know that my Husband will be dressing in my clothes when I'm at work."

Mind you, knowing my luck, I would find someone who was keen to extend invitations and friendship; to include us in a gathering where my husband could relax and be Herself.

Because you never know who is also hiding the secret.

You can see our dilemma, even my Husband found it impossible to expect public acceptance and consequently wished Zabina was not "real." Even today, with gender equality, cross-dressing is rarely accepted fully.

It is the hidden gender. Any person in any street can be a cross-dresser, hiding their own demons behind the identity they were born with. And let's not forget, ultimately enjoying who they are.

Which brings my own identity and image into question. Influenced by the swinging 60's, yes, it was that long ago, I exhibited the waif like image of models from that time.

I did keto before social media told everyone else, I starved myself to stay that way before anorexia made the daily news and I wore the fashions as they moved from stilettos to kitten heels, platforms and back again.

I loved to be seen as representative of our generation and I grafted hard to be that way. That is partly why my Husband noticed me.

I couldn't have known that he also chose me out of admiration for my style, envy for my freedom to be innovative; finally, amazement at my subtle skill with black eyeliner and red lipstick.

I enjoyed my distinctive appearance, savoured how my body felt in the tight, short clothes of the era; mostly, I enjoyed the shoes.

So, it came as no surprise to me that cross-dressers get a lot of kicks from their craft. If only it didn't affect my relationship with the man I had admired for his muscles and tight trousers. I felt cheated, as I appreciate men who look good because they are men.

How I had loved the glam rock and tight jeans of the 70's. Even saw the appeal of the pretty boy 80's. Including the eyeliner and big hair, the metamorphosis of male image over the decades.

But this was not enough for my Husband.

Perhaps if my own style had not been so strong, my sense of identity not so contemporary, I would have found my Husband's invasion into my world a little less threatening. Less competitive.

He found it hard to believe that I found myself in competition with Zabina, surely it was a compliment to choose me, to copy my excellence with the current look? But this was my look, not his.

"I could never look as good as you," he stated. "I'm a bloke."

"You don't say," I said, yet again. "Who'd have thought it, eh?"

Again, he didn't quite grasp the humour.

31

And The World Keeps Turning

Throughout this autobiography, for that is what it is, I have loved my Husband and I will always continue to do so, whatever the conclusion of our adventure.

Many book reviewers complain about the lack of empathy towards the cross-dresser, with some publications being labelled as "man-hating" and one sided.

I hope I can do better than that.

I hope I can explain our story, telling it as it was with the empathy and understanding that we both deserve, without boring you with day to day management of our own normal.

The world keeps turning, taking with it our tiny, insignificant lives. In the big scheme, this is no massive deal.

My Husband told me that recent events had really helped; that he no longer needed to dress. He'd got it "out of his system" and was ready to move on. I think he truly believed that he was "cured"; as if he had taken a course of antibiotics which changed the outcome.

I was too scared to believe a word of it, mostly because of my own evidence based research and that of the medical profession.
And after all, not only had I met Zabina, I KNEW Zabina.

However, I was too tired to resist.
And anyway, the glitter and cheap stilettos seemed to be gone, at least for now, so who was I to argue?

Months went by, perhaps longer. I don't even recall the time-frame. We were doing well. My Husband had recently changed jobs and I was progressing nicely with my own career.

I was taking residential courses, often away for weeks on end. My Husband was always pleased to welcome me home with a smile.

He was equally content to see me off on the next course, with the unnecessary assurance that Zabina was not in residence anymore.

I put any pointless concerns out of my head.

32

Becoming very committed to my new ventures, perhaps selfishly, thoughtlessly, I put my Husband's alter ego where maybe, she belonged. I almost, but never fully, dared to feel that I was happy.

Having not totally recovered, I was still struggling with the image I once had, not quite able to appreciate that I could still carry off the persona of a style icon. Maybe denial kept me away from the coveted, glamorous reflection I once wore with such confidence.

I also admit that I had allowed good living to take over. In short, I had started to get fat, certainly in my own eyes. This did not feel good and I found that the mirror, on this occasion, did not lie.
I was not looking at my best.

My husband, maybe out of genuine thought or maybe out of politeness, told me that I still looked beautiful and that he would always love me, no matter how I looked. The statement bore an ironic twist which was not wasted on either of us.

I decided to shelve the weight gain "for now," basking in this newfound life of contentment, of love and personal success. There were other, more important issues to consider at this time and after all, we had never been the type to take numerous photos which could betray the departure of my former self, albeit only temporary.

I am grateful that it was before the time of selfies and social media.

We were leading interesting and enjoyable lives which again allowed independent and separate activities. My husband went out for the evening to meet friends and I settled down for a quiet evening of indulgence with some lone TV of my choice.

A phone call took away my attention, when a friend from a recent work course asked if I could send images for an article about our success. I grimaced at the thought that recent photos of me would be shared publicly, but it was a good advert for the project.

I could not find the photos. Sifting through folders, I found nothing. I did find a solution, but my delight was short lived. On clicking search, I was unaware of the regret that I would feel, forever after.

In the search box, I had typed
.jpeg

33

Stolen

And there she was, in all her glory.

Little point in asking who, for you know as well as I, that it was
Zabina who looked back from those thumbnail images.
Hundreds and hundreds of tiny pictures.

From the filenames, I knew that these had come my own camera
and they were now housed within my own computer.

I was right about the wig. Along with the makeup, it did, indeed,
complete the transformation.

I was transfixed.
I didn't know whether to be fascinated or ill.

To see Zabina staring back at me was shocking, as in, it was
unexpected. The gallery was also shocking, simply because of the
level of transformation.

I looked systematically through the list of photographs.
Head shots, smiling shyly, loving the camera, flicking the hair.
Very obviously my Husband.
"He needs some help with that makeup," I mused.

Head and shoulders came next, turning, posing, different outfits. I
wondered how many hours and days these shots must have taken,
looking objectively at what lay before my eyes, almost life-sized on
the screen in front of me.

It was obvious that the full length shots were taken in the same
lengthy shoot, as the hair and makeup were exact. This time, the
outfits, always high necked and long sleeved, had a knee length
leather skirt and stilettos, black tights, followed by a change of
outfit with a short, short, denim skirt. To my dismay, the tights
were stockings, held up with suspenders.

The final set of shots stopped me dead in my tracks..
Glamour poses pouted from the screen, loving the camera with a
distinct edge of pure sleaze in scanty undergarments.

I was horrified, for the clothes, underwear and shoes, were all mine.

Just A Normal Day

We're not great ones
For taking snapshots
Of our life

But one day
Searching for a particular image
I typed in .jpeg

Apparently it's quite common
This need to take snapshots

"To see what I looked like," you said

Forgive me if I don't feel the need
For a photoshoot
Each morning before work

HER, demure
HER, pouting
HER, smiling
HER

Like a low class glamour model
Glaring from the pages
Feigning sexuality
Which used to be mine

Just another normal bloke
On a normal day?

Aftermath

Now, there was no going back.

If I ever doubted that this was with us for life, there was no doubt in my mind now.
But at least we knew where we stood, the full visual force of it all.

In some ways I felt better, though the shock of seeing the physical enormity of this change in my Husband would stay with me forever.

I had been living in a mixed state of hope, fear and expectation for far too long, but now I knew that my research was correct and most (but take heart, not all) men in my Husband's situation will want to go further than any activities they may admit to. It is likely that if they surrender to temptation, lies will ensue to spare the aftermath.

You may see this as an admirable deception to keep me sane.

But the revelation simplified my situation, my line of thought.
I could stay; live with Zabina. Or someone could leave.

Of course, that thought was not the first thing that came to mind. I'm sure you can imagine what the next few hours meant for me and the emotions which went round and round and round, spiralling from calmness to pure, out of control crazy.

I was actually calmer than I believed possible. Because the rages of the past had already vented at the problem, the cause, the general effect and the even the ultimate choices.

But this was a chilling calmness from within, the revelation of what it actually meant for me. Beyond Zabina.

I felt violated. We had already gone through the betrayal, the other woman, feeling unimportant, unattractive and second best.

This time, I did not blame Zabina.

For it was my Husband who had taken my clothes, **his** disregard of how I might feel about such misuse of personal, intimate garments.

As with no thought at all, he had given them away to Zabina.

I heard his key in the door.

I remained silent, which was the first thing that worried him.

Never had I felt so ugly, unwanted, unattractive and yes, fat.
How dare he fit into my clothes better than I did.
Red, red, control the red mist......

I had been crying, which is never a good look.

Not needing to say a word, because he knew, he had guessed, for
what else could it be, I looked towards the computer screen and
nodded in the general direction of the corner desk.

As my Husband touched the mouse, Zabina, in full glory, complete
with sexual pose and sensuous pout, jumped onto the screen.

It wasn't quite as good as the deodorant and socks episode, but
enough to make him step back quickly.

"Probably to get a better look and admire Herself," I thought drily.

He had been drinking. Full of bravado and alcohol, he started with
the drivel which justified the scenario.

"Just don't," I said. "Grow up. I don't want any excuses.
This is not normal. Why did you use my clothes and why, on earth,
did you use MY camera and MY computer? Are you stupid?"

He shifted uneasily on the shiny floor, from flat boot to flat boot.
Evidence of his good night out with the boys stood out like a
beacon, with curry and beer stains discolouring his very male jeans.

He tried the coy Zabina look, but for some reason, it didn't have the
desired effect. It must have been the clothes he was wearing.

"So," I continued. "When was it and why? It must have taken an
age to put all that stuff on and take those photos."

Somehow, by a slim margin, he survived his next action.

Before replying, he glanced directly at Zabina on the screen, as if
asking for Her permission to answer.

So, what was it that made my Husband defy his assurance that
Zabina was no longer around?
Why did he go to such great lengths to provide proof of how
unappealing and disagreeable Her presence could be in my life?

It was difficult to believe that this was happening, after all the
talking and soul-searching we had done in recent times. I had
asked, time and time again, if there was more that I should know. I
had extended the hand of acceptance to Zabina, allowing Her into
my home; albeit it with discretion and moderation.

Feeling the right to be more than a little aggrieved, I waited for
answers. My expression clearly stated that lies were not an option.

Apparently, my acceptance of Zabina, though not exactly inviting
her to Sunday lunch, had curbed the rebellion – let's reflect on the
girlfriend who encouraged my Husband to dress and go out. Simply
being invited had again reduced Zabina's voracious appetite.

Herein, the psyche of the cross-dresser was further revealed.
My husband had considered himself "cured" because he loved me
and no longer needed Zabina. Each time I went away, he felt that
he did not need Her because he felt secure, loved, fulfilled; with me.

But my Husband became bored when I was away. Not content with
doing something remotely useful, like gardening, he decided to visit
Zabina, who was, of course, delighted to escape from the closet.

Apparently, once she was "up and running" it was difficult to stop.
And with each layer that was added, it didn't feel right not to "do it
properly" and continue to the full works.

"And the photographs? Why did you keep them on the computer?"
"Well," he replied, " I couldn't see properly in the mirror and I
needed to see what I looked like.
Maybe part of me wanted to get caught. As I couldn't tell you."

"So, when I was on my course and you used to call and say you
were missing me, were you dressed as Her?"

"Sometimes," came the reply.

I was not sick, but my stomach resisted as I held my dinner down.

38

Moving Forward Forever

Now I knew all the facts, exactly what I was dealing with, strangely, some things, at least, got easier.

Don't get me wrong.
I was shocked to the core and had no idea how to absorb all that I had seen, or indeed, what I was going to do about it.

Of the two options of should I stay or should one of us leave, I felt too fragile to deal with the ultimate decision. I did choose to stay, for now, after deciding that I should break things into small decisions and take control of my own part.

Sometimes, when you are faced with the worst scenario, it is easier to see the good, nestling in the corner. You are no longer blinded by fear of the unknown.

My Husband, too, calmed down. He had been caught out like a naughty child but was now faced with the responsibility of his own actions. They were his choices.

We had discussed the violation of my privacy, how I expected him to get his own clothes; that he owed it to us both to keep Zabina in Her place, where She did not interfere with our relationship.
In return, I accepted Her existence and acknowledged that he would visit Zabina's world and I would do my best to live with it.

It all sounds very simple, but once the cards were on the table, it was pointless dragging up don't know, can't help it, or won't try.
It was either that or get the hell out.

From my point of view, I had to let him be what he was, to have the freedom to be independent, out of my sight, to eat curry with his friends without me suspecting that every spare moment was spent with Zabina.

With the ease that most men have in shrugging off the awkward, my Husband quickly became happy and accepting.

For my part, the things which had been driving me mad did not go away, but they became manageable.
At least, on the surface.

We now move on in years, not days.
Some of them rolled past with hardly a blip, others had their moments. For that is normal life.

Zabina was always there in the background.
But hardly ever in my face; and that had to do.

If She did raise her head above the parapet, it was less about direct confrontation and more about the peripherals.

I would look at a family photograph and see my short haired, suited Husband staring back with the look of Zabina in his eyes. That subtle smile She saved for the camera.

At other times, the shorts would be a little too tight, the glance in the mirror a little too long and the reaction to a comment a little too vicious. And then She was gone.

The bad days were usually fuelled by alcohol; there was far too much alcohol around in those days. My husband would tend to drink just a certain amount before Zabina would get tetchy and pick a fight. For my part, I waited for the trigger point and bit hard, when my vocabulary demonstrated articulate, hard defence.

Mostly, we just settled into this phase, rubbing along together in the manner of people who were getting older together when priorities had changed. And of course, we were always aware of how fortunate we were; there were many facing illness who would relish my easy life with a cross-dresser.

But we were certainly no longer young lovers. In fact, we were barely lovers at all, which to be honest, suited us both; we both had disturbing memories to live with.

In its place, was a cemented bond that would never be broken and in the secret world of Zabina, we screamed solidarity. Indeed, our once innovative life now seemed dull in comparison and it had undeniably settled into silent, middle aged suburbia.

But there are always undercurrents.

Whilst my Husband now pottered happily through the days with his mostly "normal" pastimes, I'm afraid I still had my demons.

40

I didn't even know about some of these elephants in my room and I defy anyone to predict how and where the manifestations appeared.

Rarely did I feel haunted by Zabina and I can honestly say that genuinely, I never felt threatened by Her again. I owned my territory and could choose my own road.

What I didn't realise, what I didn't expect, was the slow pain which grew within my own body, mind and identity.

This was dismissed as the process of getting old, initially by me and always by my Husband who still said he loved me however I looked.

None of this was about Zabina. I had stopped caring about myself. Anyway, she would no longer want to borrow my clothes, for I had increased my bodyweight by 40% or six stones.

Realistically, my keto and starvation days of the 60's and 70's had kept me waiflike and on the edge of underweight.

My first experience of that lying mirror had been perceived fatness looking out from the skinny frame of a near anorexic. So, the first two stones were barely noticeable; I looked incredibly healthy.

The next increase was starting to tip the balance. The psychological effect of moving from XL normal range to the outsize rail was not unnoticed. Zabina was not alone in disliking the available fashion.

The final increase was undeniable, plus depression, self-loathing.

That old enemy, the mirror, did not even attempt to lie. I did question how Zabina nurtured Her own relationship with the oracle, which made Her feel beautiful, because I sure needed a few new tips for gazing into this glass pool which, for me, reflected only evil.

This culminated in a medical appointment. Stripped to my underwear, the doctor went through the process of blood pressure and weight gain, writing it all down. I acknowledged the problem.

"I'm sure someone loves you," he replied, glancing over with an expression which showed that he clearly did not believe this.

It was little wonder that my Husband had created Zabina.

We all have our issues, doubts.
We go on bravely, day to day, as if nothing is happening. Truthfully, most of the time, nothing out of the ordinary is happening, because it is normal to get old, overweight and sometimes a little down.

That is when we need someone. Someone who will listen, say the right things, even when what comes out is not the expected topic.

As we know, that was going to be difficult. So, I said nothing.

I was having some issues at work. In a public facing role, I was good at what I did and the clients loved the way I worked. I was popular. But as is often the case, my face was a little out of place where management were concerned and I could do nothing right.

It was bound to fall apart, but not in the expected manner.

These were days before annual staff appraisals, but we occasionally got a grilling on why we had carried out our daily roles the way we had. It wouldn't be allowed to happen in the same way now.

There was no denying that I had not been performing as well of late and had recently been on sick leave. Stress is what we call it now.

"This has happened before, hasn't it?" I was asked. I nodded.
"This can't go on. Either things improve or we have to look at your position here. Is there anything else affecting the situation that I should know about?"

Panic rose …… him or me; *him or me*; **HER or me** ………… ????

For the first time, publicly ……… ME ……

The words spilled out like twelve pint vomit.
Once I started, the words would not stop; my employer simply stared in disbelief at the things that had happened to me.

As I dried my eyes and stood up, preparing to meet my next client, my boss tried to stop me – "No, you can't go out like that, it's not fair. I'll take the appointment."

He looked on in further disbelief, as I stood tall, with a smile on my face. I carried on and did what I was paid to do; my job was safe.

I didn't tell my Husband about the incident for quite a long time. When I did, he was appalled. "You told him what? About me? Well, that's stopped any social gatherings from your place of work then," he spat sarcastically.

The old dry humour engaged, as I thought, "It wasn't about you, it was about Zabina. Because it always comes back to Zabina." But I curbed the reply. I was no longer shocked; acceptance had quietened my responses to the things I could not change.

Forgive me for talking a little less about Zabina for now; for allowing a little indulgence in what was to become my own lowest ebb. The path we take will sometimes be a dark one. If you, too, are living this life, be sure that I feel your pain, in times when perhaps, there is no-one else who can listen, no-one else who may speak.

It is why I write this book; I am with you all. The three of you.

But there is only so much that you can bear, watching your once confident self, falling far from the tree.

On the upside, my employer treated me very differently for the rest of my career within his sector. I became more successful at work and actually secured a new job, in a new town.

From here, my own story moves sideways, albeit temporarily.

And I was to be away from home for at least five days a week.

I appreciate your sharp intake of breath, perhaps wondering at the absurdity of why I dared to leave my Husband alone for so long?

Or maybe you applaud that at last, Zabina was free to be Herself?

But I needed to save myself to have any chance of saving our marriage. For I had nothing left to give.

My Husband had mixed feelings. Didn't we all.
We knew where his solitude would lead, but we also knew that we both needed a chance.

I took the secondment and every scrap of my clothing went with me. I returned each weekend, carrying, at most, a small suitcase.

43

City Life

I loved it. I loved the challenges of a totally different environment.

The respect that I earned, simply for being me, restored my self-respect. I was still fat, but I became glamourous fat.
And the restaurants were rather good; I could not blame Zabina.

Deciding that I would stay for at least a couple of years, I took a permanent position. When my expenses stopped, my Husband went into financial panic, requesting that I come home.
I had always intended to go back home. Just not yet.

I'd always fancied a mobile home and it seemed the ideal opportunity to get a holiday retreat for the future, but one which I could make my own and live in for now.

My Husband reverted to type. Or should I say "tight."
He scoured every newspaper, magazine and even estate agents, in an attempt to secure the best deal for every penny.

Meanwhile, I found a lovely site, out of town and near the river. An old, but serviceable mobile home was found and at the right price.

Now, in those days, before the huge leisure parks with pools and bars, saunas and spas, there were large fields, with generators and water containers. My desired home was little more than a lined out porta cabin, with a foldout bed. A rather splendid portable toilet was housed in a tiny washroom, where a hip bath sat in a tight corner, with a rubber hosed shower head connected to the taps.

A rather good two burner hob, tiny oven and gas fridge made up the kitchenette, with some rather snazzy red cupboards, clearly from the previous era, making up the difference between caravan and mobile home. The gas bottle sat on laid slabs, outside the door.

My Husband was having none of it. He found an old wreck, in the corner of a farmyard, at a tenth of the price. It was filthy, with a camp bed at one end. The caravan, which was in no way a mobile home, was simply too small to be described as having another end. A camping stove lay in a corner, next to a plastic washing up bowl.

"It'll do," he said. "Would it do for Zabina?" I asked with interest.

44

400 Square Feet

Oh, how I loved my new home. 400 square feet of me.
I adored the whole thing and after scrubbing and polishing my
world, I added rugs and bright curtains, a futon in the centre
section, where there was space to breathe and practice yoga.

The red kitchenette performed well, cooking up simple meals on a
whim and the gas fridge cooled wine and beer, ready for my daily
return to this bohemian, sunlit palace.
When the weather was kind, my chair was moved outside and onto
the slabbed area of solitude. Not quite a patio, but close enough.

I was no longer alone, for I had my world to keep me company.
Offers to socialise were lovely, but mostly, I relished my own space,
which was filled with books and an old TV, which had no remote
control, but total choice of media exposure.

My Husband rarely visited.

Logistically, it was easier for me to travel home, where we would
meet up with friends and appear to be a well-adjusted, happy pair.

Most of them probably thought we were a little mad for this strange
lifestyle. We had not quite reached the decade where people were
comfortable in leaving their husbands to cope alone. This was, of
course, mostly from the viewpoint of my Husband's male friends.

I do realise that perhaps selfishly, I have no idea to this day what
he ate, or how he looked after himself, but he was not unhappy.

I spent my weekends catching up with my washing, which went
straight into the machine on entering the house. There was little
that would interest Zabina, but I wasn't taking chances. My clean
underwear was packed away and placed straight back into my own
car boot as soon as it was dry. This left only the single suitcase in
our place of residence. The case was locked with a little silver key.

Bystanders would find this a weird way to live. But no-one knew. By
Sunday, I felt doubly homesick.

Stay here, in our shared home, or return there, to my own domain?
    I was never sure from which direction I was drawn the most.

I always appreciated the silence, as solitude embraced my return with the fragrant smell of nothing but me and my clean washing.

And the absence of Her.

That's how I absorbed it, this thing which freed me totally.

I was absent from the air which tainted our shared home.
On entering the house, I regularly became aware of a subtle smell, a musty fragrance of not so clean clothes and cheap perfume.

Opening windows never quite removed the bouquet of Zabina.

I continued to drive to the house each weekend for over a year and this suited us both perfectly. But after a hard winter and a few breakdowns, my Husband offered to share the travel burden.

It was lovely to see him and he admired the way that I had furnished the mobile home. He seemed to have got over the financial panic of buying into it, although I'm not quite sure if I ever forgave him for suggesting that offer of alternative accommodation.

We settled into a fortnightly routine, one weekend in the house, so that I could do my washing and the next weekend away. We used my little haven as the holiday home for which it was intended.

My Husband started to settle in and feel at home, which was good, wasn't it? But I couldn't help feeling that he was invading my space, changing the ambience of the room where I felt most as home.

I shelved the feeling, thinking how selfish I had become. Until that was, when he commented how "relaxed" he felt in my little world.

A chill spread through me and I fought the red mist which ensued.

"You wouldn't bring Zabina here would you? Not to my space?"
"It's my space too," he snarled. "No, I would never do that to you."
I saw the twitch of the jaw, unease in his eyes. The lie.

Much later, under cover of darkness and with the spare keys to my Husband's car still in my hand, the boot clicked open.

The sickly sweet fragrance of Zabina wafted out into the night.

46

400 Square Feet

Less than 400 square feet
Where I go to be alone

Alone
Whilst She prowls my domain
My house, once my home
The predator who stole
My life, my identity
And even my clothes

I asked you never to bring Her here

She dominates
Dark corners of my life
But you invited Her here
Regardless of me

Though She never left the car
You brought Her with hopeful intent
Always keeping Her close

"It's my space too" you said

Like my house was my space
Before it was Hers?
Where the walls cry out Her memory
As stiletto heels echo
Like ghosts in the night

Just like the first time
Red mist

No, beyond the first time
Glowing, white hot
Screaming at me
To put an end
To this misery

When I smelt Her presence
Rising like a breath
From the boot of the car
That first bad memory
Only a threshold away

400 square feet
Still intact and sacred
For now

Just 400 square feet
Such a small thing to beg
From the size of the world

And yet
You would still deny
This tiny space

400 square feet

And Again

And again ………. And again ……….

It really came as no surprise.
Reassuringly, I was in a different place and was more myself again.
Although my Husband may not have agreed that this was beneficial.

It made a difference to me.

This time I was well equipped to handle the situation and did so
with total efficiency. Quite simply, he would go home next morning,
taking the contents of the boot with him.

My need was ruthless, craving space.
From Her. But mostly from my Husband.

Not only would he not bring her here again, but he would not be
coming here again unless there was a very good reason.

We reverted to our previous arrangement and I returned to the
house each weekend. Only in hindsight did I see that I must have
looked like a frightened refugee, clutching my small suitcase, it's
tiny silver key hanging around my neck as if my life depended on it.

I added a small caveat to our agreement – should I choose to stay
in my home, the mobile home, for the odd weekend, I would not be
pressured into going back to our house, or the domestic bliss within.

He left next morning, looking guilty. I said little.

I did not return to the house for a month. Angrier than I had ever
felt in my life, I needed time for this latest betrayal to sink in.

My Husband was devastated. Whether this was from loss of my
company or from being caught out, I will never fully know.
He begged me to return and to get another job, closer to "home."

Still fuming, I said he could accept it, or quite simply, we could
discuss amicable arrangements and one of us could leave.

Leave the house, of course.
I was not letting go of my home for anyone, least of all Zabina.

The thing that never ceases to amaze me is how the human mind recovers, accepting life's traumas and allowing us to show solidarity as if all is normal.

We still breathed, slept when exhausted. As things settled down and I returned to the house, albeit sporadically, no-one, the ever present no-one, could have known exactly what had happened.

Our independent lifestyles did, of course, cause suspicion amongst our number. Friends started to ask if anything was wrong. Why was I away so much? Was there someone else?
I should add that it was mostly the wives of my Husband's friends who asked. My own friends were probably developing an instinct.

And so, we began the next phase of the silence.
Probably the worst one. The one where I could not defend my actions because the reasons were taboo.

I spent a lot of time thinking about the answers I had to give.
The repercussions came, intermittent but hard and fast in their nature. People had clearly started to see this as my fault.

I remember a particular social weekend, where my Husband complained of a stiff neck. One such acquaintance offered a neck massage, berating me with the information that he was "really stressed, don't you ever do this? Being stressed isn't good for him, you know. Poor thing."

I held my thoughts. They were not wasted, but certainly not on her. "Get your own house in order," said my mind. "What do you know? He knows exactly how to relax."

My Husband lapped up the attention, with Zabina in his eyes. No support was offered in my defence. Poor, poor things that They are.

Who cared about *my* stress?

Even my own friends started to question my motives, though mostly out of consideration for me. At the beginning, at least.
But I was shutting them out of my life and they did not know why. As they could never know.

For the first time, I began to feel alone during my precious solitude.

The solid veneer, our front of house, remained intact.

As ever, life was not all bad, or perhaps it is my insistence on glass half full which keeps me sane. At least, most of the time.

My Husband continued in whatever manner he chose and probably considered himself to be fortunate in living his pseudo life at will. Even if it were only when I was absent.

Despite criticism from others, we both knew that there were benefits all round in having our own parallel universe.
If nothing else, we had time to assess ourselves.

Most marriages require patience, learning how to intertwine two lives, how the circles coincide. Ours required a different skill.

The circles of our particular existence were unable to move freely amongst others. Our worlds were not so pliable and we were bonded at strategic points, places where flexibility was not an option; secrecy; protection; understanding.

Secrets and protection were undeniable advantages to us both, but I was under no illusion that this was mostly for my Husband's benefit. Understanding was mostly one sided. I was expected to recognise my Husband's needs, but he merely tolerated any constraint.

Examining these points, I became aware of the level of inequality in our oh, so modern relationship. I had been blinded.

My own survival, ensconced in the warmth of my bohemian palace, offered a reclusive, charmed life of sorts. My liberation was offered unexpectedly, through the acceptable avenue of job opportunity.

I had always been comfortable in my own company, needing no-one. But how would I react to feeling deserted, unwanted, abandoned, like my Husband, who so craved approval for Zabina?

This epiphany moment pulled my inner vision into sharp focus. In seeking solace, in giving space to us all, I was mistaken in thinking that we had learned to live with our issue.

We had merely learnt to live independently of each other.

Life has a habit of moving things around when you least expect it. I had another year of bohemian living before the next major change arrived on our doorstep.

It wasn't the easiest year. With the best will in the world, long distance commuting wears you out. It puts strain on your quality of life, your bank balance and as the miles clock up, your car tyres.

Living in two places has a strange effect. Though you have wistful moments of longing for whichever home is furthest away, the pull of now becomes comfortable, the tiredness of the journey catches up and you realise that you are not getting any younger.

But then I received devastating news that the field, my field, the acres of my beautiful home, was to be sold. Completely out of the blue. I didn't know what to say; what to do. My Husband had stopped asking me to come back permanently. He said I should decide for myself, as my job was near "the caravan."

Moving the structure was impossible, it was too old to withstand any journey. I was offered compensation of much more than its value, more than it was sensible to refuse.

Crying didn't help as I sat at my work desk with a desolate air. Logically, I could rent somewhere else, it was by no means a lifelong disaster, but at this point it felt like one.

I received a lot of support from my colleagues, who, after all, had helped me to find my current haven and would help me again. Three months' notice gave ample time to find a solution.

But coincidences sometimes happen, all at once and very quickly.

Just two days later, a newspaper was placed on my desk, a red ring around an advert for a position within a short distance of our house.

To cut a long story very short, surprisingly, I got the position.

With a partially heavy heart, two months later, I was heading back. My smiling husband was waiting at the door to welcome me home. It was as though I had never been away.

And no-one was any the wiser.

Home Again

To start with, I missed my little world.

To be honest, things felt slightly overwhelming, but my Husband had worked hard to make sure that I had a good homecoming and he was nothing if not attentive. At times it got a little stifling, as I had been accustomed to more solitude, but I had different things to deal with, such as a new job.

I only had a few days before work took over and I didn't have time to dwell on issues. I decided to put historic problems to the back of my mind and enjoy the life I had.

For the next few months, we trod carefully around each other. It was summer and we had reconnected fully with our friends. It was natural for them to assume that we had gone through a bad patch and things were now back to normal and as they should be.

My Husband seemed happy, as indeed did I. Zabina had not been seen or heard.

I was genuinely curious about how he had been coping and asked how he was feeling about my return.

He was honest. Zabina had roamed her lair at will in my absence. As expected, to start with, the thrill of being the Lady of the house had resulted in daily dressing, experimenting. He suggested that I would be impressed at the improvement in Her appearance.

I'm not denying that an old chill went through my body on hearing this, but I had not returned in order to fight. I allowed him to continue in peace, simply nodding, listening to his words.

Having not been present at any point during these activities, it was less shocking and actually interesting, almost as if I was listening to a stranger's story. In some ways, of course, this is exactly what it was. Because for the past few years, my Husband's life in our house had been lived as the exotic interloper, Zabina, whenever he chose.

I had not seen Zabina in the flesh since I moved into the mobile home, to my bohemian world where life became so different. In fact, I had not seen Her at all since discovering the photographs.

My Husband continued with his story.
After the initial elation of self-indulgence, the usual decline followed and it became too much effort for him to get dressed up and put on makeup. I could identify with that.

"There is one thing," he said, in the inevitable "I want more" voice. "I'd really like to go out dressed like it. Would you come with me?"

"Where were you thinking of going?" I replied, surprised that the words came out sounding so reasonable.
There's no denying that the old mist was rising quietly.

He had found a gathering, which occurred once a month at a large Hotel, just off the motorway. Somewhere discreet with easy parking and a bar. We could stay overnight. I couldn't help imagining a seedy motel, more used to the illicit.

I freaked inwardly, but I had returned home, knowing the reasons why I had screamed for space. I stayed calm.
"I don't think I'm ready to do that," I replied steadily.

"OK," said my Husband, "Would you mind if I went on my own?"

I shrugged. And as though he had simply asked if I wanted a cup of tea, my Husband moved on, suggesting that we "go to the pub for a drink and see everyone."

"If only they *could* see you," I thought drily.
Obviously, my Husband's next plan had been carefully hatched and all I could do was wait for the evidence.

But in fact, I don't think he ever went there. If he did, I never knew. He claimed that it was a great idea, but when the moment came, he "couldn't be bothered." This was probably true. I came to understand that unless Zabina was in the spotlight of shock and surprise, She really wasn't as keen.

Occasionally, we would talk about Zabina like she was an exotic maiden aunt, only appearing at weddings and funerals and with an edge of dare, the curious, neither which could be curtailed.

It may sound strange, but as long as Zabina was not actually in the room, I was somehow able to almost accept Her flamboyance.

It is fair to say that life, overall, was good.
We had a reasonable income, a lovely home and great friends. Our jobs suited us well and our time apart had created two, at least partially, well-adjusted and independent people.

Any issues of my own were mostly just that and if I was haunted, it was from my own ghosts.

Until a routine doctor's appointment placed a new strand into the woven thread. Forced me to consider alternate shadows.

A workplace medical, a fact of life in a newly caring industry.
I was nervous and I had never forgotten the last medical, which reminded me that I was no longer young or attractive.

I knew I could do better. I was drinking too much; a victim of a successful life, or so I thought. And I was still too fat.
A slighter shadow than before, but still fat.

This appointment could not have been more different. The doctor was a breath of fresh air to my inner hysteria and the medical part was respectfully dismissed with little more than a warning that as we age, we can no longer overplay life's excesses without reproach.

I was acquitted. Until the contemporary style of this new age care delved a little deeper into what we now know as mental health.

I was asked if anything else was bothering me, anything which troubled me. "Other than being fat, feeling second best?" I replied. "And why do you feel that way?" was the catalyst.

Out it came, in waves of glory, like a West End show that had never been aired. The doctor listened intently; Then changed my outlook.

"You owe it to yourself to care for your own wellbeing," came the feedback. "How can you expect to nurture others if you are not content within your own skin? And that includes the subconscious."

The remark changed my life forever.
It was time to cultivate my own needs. Not to run away, but to face the demons, defend my identity.

Embrace the Nemesis.

And so began the transformation from me to me.

I did ease off a little, tried a bit of a health kick, lost a dress size, nearly two. "That was careless," quipped my Husband. His sarcasm provoked the unkind thought that he was probably sizing up the clothes for Zabina's own middle aged girth.

I've always been an extremist. I have dark thoughts of doubt, I am scared of the world, but I also have a desperate need to be an extrovert when the switch is on. My momentum is preserved by being excessive, for if I stop, the moment is gone, the effort is wasted and I return to my natural reclusive state to recover.

It came as little surprise to me when I went off the rails. Heavily. It had been coming for years and I saw it as my last chance to shine like the diamond I once was.

I started to diet, sensibly. Hell, it was awful, all that thinking about what I ate made me more obsessively hungry. I dreamed of food, of recipes, but in the middle of the night there was no healthy focus.

Having found myself some new friends on the decidedly dodgy side of fun, I had taken to late night partying on school nights and all night drinking at weekends. Always the ladette before it was fashionable, my Husband chose to abstain from my poor behaviour. "*My poor behaviour?* Ha, ha, now there's a thought," I giggled.

Going back to the terrible habits of my youth sparked a 60's memory of thin. Don't eat. Or eat nothing but steak. And that's what I did. Luckily, not for long. And lucky or not, endless units of alcohol kept my intake high enough to avert anorexic decline.

Once the cravings stopped and a form of high energy hysteria took over, I lost almost three stones in eight weeks. Adding to this the carelessly mislaid dress sizes, I had discarded four stones in total.

I felt marvellous, wonderful. To be honest, I looked pretty good for a nearly old lady. I was actually the healthy weight I needed to be and had now re-kindled my relationship with the medium sized clothes that I had preserved with eternal hope.

My impressive cleavage did not go away, the slim hips returned. My heels, both historically and now, remained higher than Zabina's.

I was wildly out of control. With the skill of a professional fraudster, somehow I held it together and coped with it all.

That didn't make it right.
I had teamed up with an old friend from the City, who was nothing if not rebellious. Very alpha male, I felt safe, protected.

We prowled the City streets at night, in places to which I would not dare. I followed in his wake like a gangster's moll, striding alongside in the manner to which stilettos were invented to impress.

This carried on for several weeks when I hardly returned home. At which point, I did consider how much longer my body, especially my liver, could keep up with this lifestyle.
Oh, what memories we made. But I went home to clean up.

My Husband didn't seem to be too bothered about anything I did. I wasn't trying to shock, but he showed no reaction at all. I suspect that in my absence, Zabina also strode around like a gangster's moll, though less elegantly and on parquet, not the City streets.

If only things had settled down, but we had a little further to go before that could happen.

It came as a shock to me, but should have been more obvious, that a confident, older woman would command some sort of attention. And not only of the outraged, critical kind.

My final escapade was less City glamour and more Village fete. I formed a friendship with a veteran gent of portly stature, whose late life crisis overtook my own.

We drank real ale in backstreet pubs, attended local events and generally discussed the downside of life. It was not the most exciting phase of my regeneration, but its contrast was a welcome relief. And I did feel glamourous in the surrounding company.

This was fine, until he decided that it was time to leave his wife and out of the blue, told her the same. I felt as if I were in a mad world, where at any second, the village cafe would proclaim, with insane normality, that it was time for tea.

I ran from this tale of delusion and back to the near normal Zabina.

I Don't Know Why

Who am I? I used to know, I never questioned why
I knew the rules by which we lived, I didn't have to try
And then my world came crashing down as if the sky did fall
The only thing I'm sure of is I don't want this at all

Is there a choice? Did I believe that I could change a thing
Why did you have to tell of all the heartache it would bring?
But would I want to live a lie? I have a right to know
At least I have the chance to choose if I should stay or go

I know that choice you'll never have, you cannot walk away
There's nothing I can do to help, there's nothing I can say
I do admire your honesty, your torment I can see
But often, still, I have to ask, "Why did you pick on me?"

You never seem to choose me, there's always something new
You're always so distracted, always something else to do
I know it's me who understands, the only one to care
Or was it me, the only one who offered to be there?

Then suddenly, you need me and yes, I'm always here
As if I'm never terrified, with nothing left to fear
I just don't think you understand the chill I feel inside
The worries that I have for you, this life we have to hide

I can't confide in others, no, I cannot tell a friend
I can't reveal the other you for risk She would offend
You can't believe the solitude, the help that isn't there
I'm torn between the three of us despite how much I care

It nearly drove me crazy; It drove me to deceive
It drove me to betrayal; Even then, I couldn't leave
I don't know where this life will end, I know you feel it too
I only know one certain thing - This love I have for you

And in return, the love you have for me we can't deny
In answer to the questions, well, I guess we have to try
And so, we stay together, seems we just don't want to go
But let's not ask the question why this is, I just don't know

Facing The Nemesis

Getting back to near normal was somewhat of a relief.

I was tired, worn out, beaten.
It was as if every fibre of my being had been wrung out like a worn dishcloth and I had neither the inclination nor the strength to fight anymore.

Coming home to heal, again, was the best solution.
My husband left me mostly to my own thoughts and was not without a good measure of guilt for his part in the masquerade.

In many ways it was over. The passion, the pain of fighting for one's own cause, when truly there was no cause for conflict, had come full circle.

It was time to be at peace with each other and the world. In days gone by it was OK to take on crusades of the heart, but now, we were ever close to retirement age and needed a pillow of understanding and support on which to rest.

Which was how, after a couple of months of recuperation, we began a new conversation.

My husband was mortified by the consequences of his inner conflict, but he was also powerless to stop his craving for this harmless, non-harmless alter ego. Zabina was as much a part of his makeup as the man who left the house in work boots every day.

We talked, reminiscing, laughing, even a few tears along the way. We added a pinch of realisation to more than a few glasses of wine, for life is not always about excitement, achievement or want.

My Husband had found a new avenue to explore, a safe house which was not public but would allow him to reveal Zabina gently. A place where there was support for cross-dressers, but mainly, there was support for their wives.

He did not expect me to attend but asked if I would mind if he went. "I want to try and understand what I am."

"I'll come with you," came the surprising answer. "Let's face this."

60

We set out on the journey which would bring the most enlightening, heart-breaking and bizarrely, the most enjoyable event of my life. Don't get me wrong and especially if this is also your path, please don't think that it will solve all the issues in your world, because you will be sadly disappointed.

But there are little pockets of life tucked away in magical corners. If you can increase the sphere of your vision, there are times when you begin to understand why things are simply the way they are. Even if only for a short time, the complications are removed and you can embrace the moment with clarity.

There just happened to be a gathering on the first weekend after my Husband tentatively mentioned that we might like to go along. He was happy to wait until the next one, but I was never one to drag my heels once my mind was made up.

"Let's do it," I said, maybe with a little apprehension in my undertones. "What, really? This weekend?" replied my Husband, with more than a hint of terror displayed in the numerous undercurrents of elation, hope and ultimately, the fear of facing his demons in both myself and Zabina.

Quite simply, that is how we moved on, how we came to witness others dealing with this strange pastime. But mostly, we learned to accept a patient ear, when no other comfort could be trusted.

We planned carefully. What should either of us wear?
We agreed it was probably a good idea for me to choose my Husband's outfit and there was no denying that makeup was best left to an expert. "You are not going out wearing bright blue eyeshadow, shiny tights and a floral frock," I stated.

"That's not my style or yours," he smiled. "well, at least, not the floral frock." For the first time, we actually shared the joke.

What I should wear was also a point of debate. What was expected of me? "Don't forget," he said, "they are just normal blokes."

As usual, I struggled with this image of normal, then reconsidered. "What the hell, if they want tight jeans and cleavage, so be it."

Therefore, I wore the highest and finest stilettos in the room.

When the evening came, we were incredibly and equally nervous. I felt as if I should offer to drive, but on this occasion, my Husband offered and anyway, I did not feel ready to forego the much needed glass of wine.

When I left the house, I looked as glamorous as age and body allowed, ensuring that I did not cross the mutton dressed as lamb borderline; the jeans were dark and well fitted, the makeup understated, the cleavage just enough; the heels were exquisite and sinful.

My Husband also wore jeans, but the accessories were purely male. He carried a small sports holdall, which somehow contained over six feet of the complete Zabina, plus heels. He would enter and leave the gathering as himself, only inviting Zabina to emerge once the doors were closed firmly behind us.

As we drove, we discussed how the evening might progress, with a mixture of jubilation, fear and uncertainty. We knew where we were going, what time to be there and that we would have a private room for the transformation of Husband to Nemesis. My Husband had offered to get dressed on his own. "It won't be pleasant for you to watch," he said.

"No," I replied, "I want to see it happen, all there is to see. Anyway, I have to supervise your makeup or you'll have dark smudges and bleeding lipstick all over your face." He laughed. "And I bet you'd use blue eyeshadow. Definitely not blue," I added, with a grin.

But no-one had really told us what to expect.
When questioned about the one social gathering from his youth, my Husband either didn't or couldn't recall the order of proceedings or any mandatory etiquette. This left us somewhat unprepared.

We knew that when we were ready, we were invited to join the others who were present. We assumed they would be of like mind.

I asked how Zabina would introduce herself on entering the room. Would she speak in a lady's voice, "Hello, my name's Zabina" (high) or in my Husband's normal tone "Hello, my name's Zabina" (low)?

"I don't know," he replied.
This time, we laughed until we cried; my mascara was a mess.

Deirdre was a very kind but brave soul who let these grateful and sometimes sad, lonely, even desperate people into her home. The house was a dream come true, but I could not help wondering about her story, as she welcomed us with open arms.
Dierdre obviously had a life behind the laughter.

It was a lovely house, quite massive, five bedrooms and an amazing conservatory. It was also very private, with a sweeping driveway and a large, tree bordered garden which was not overlooked at all.

Dierdre obviously understood and as she showed my Husband to his dressing room, I was offered the choice to opt out of the next stage. But I needed to see this through, so with hidden emotion, I smiled and followed my Husband through the door and into the room.

The metamorphosis was truly fascinating, amazing, horrifying. My poor Husband was embarrassed, upset, but at the same time, uplifted and excited. This was it, the full works, as I watched him undress and start the transformation.

Starting with the clothes and from the top, the bra, this time stuffed not with tissues, but with the "chicken fillets" purchased from a back street shop. These were for an authentic look, but also, apparently, for comfort. On top of this came a plain, long sleeved, roll neck top. I had chosen the attire on the side of classy rather than sassy. After all, we had no idea how many maiden aunts would be in the room and did not want to shock or offend on a first visit.

Next came the most embarrassing part for my Husband, the special pants which held the temporarily surplus body parts out of the way, to give a flat frontal silhouette. The revered and abhorrent tights followed and before my moment of panic escalated, they were covered swiftly with a knee length, leather pencil skirt.

As my Husband was so inexperienced at applying the makeup, I actually enjoyed improving the look, with subtlety and a lifetime of skill. But I realised how lucky I was not to always need foundation.

The final, daunting moment ensued as he placed the wig that I had been dreading on his head. Zabina tossed her blonde locks freely. The stilettos were the final fragment and the Lady stood tall.

My Husband was gone.

63

With every hurdle that we cleared, the next one had always seemed bigger. But here we were and the moment had arrived.

Just as we were about to leave the room, with magical timing there was a soft knock on the door. We opened it slowly and peered out, as Dierdre whispered "Are you ready?" We both nodded.

With not quite the same impact as my evenings spent prowling the City like a gangster's moll, I strode confidently on my highest heels. I could only imagine how my Husband felt, as his stilettos tried to keep up with me and not fall down the stairs. It would not be a good entrance if he fell into a heap in the large rectangular hallway.

I had a sudden thought, an irrational fear. "I hope they know which one of us is which," ran through my mind, followed by the mental reprimand which told me to stop being either stupid or ridiculous.

The descent complete, in unison, we clicked our way across the hall and towards the large reception room. We followed Deirdre, who wore flat, sensible shoes and a very nice floral dress. She resembled a vicar's Wife at a country fete, but without the large, floppy sunhat.

To an onlooker, this scenario would have looked absurd. In fact, we laughed about it many times after the event, beginning on our journey home. It appeared that we had both felt like running away, but we also realised how difficult it would be to abscond with Zabina in tow. Anyway, the car keys were in my Husband's pocket, upstairs, where most of him currently resided in the sports holdall.

Dierdre quietly entered the reception room, where the conversation all but stopped. "Ladies," she said, "I'd like to introduce you to our new members, Zabina," she gestured towards my non-Husband with a flourish, "And," smiling broadly at me, "Her Wife, Brianna."

I swallowed deeply and smiled nervously around the room.

My initial scan took in couple of maiden aunts, sitting demurely in a corner and a perfect looking Lady, a stunning, oriental Ladyboy. But most were just like Zabina, wearing work in progress cast offs.

Suddenly, a cheery voice called, "Hello, my name's Phyllis," (low).
So now, we knew.

Immediately I understood the need for such gatherings, acknowledging the bravery of these people who might risk public ridicule if Dierdre did not open her doors; and before the evening finished, I was to understand so much more.

All eyes turned towards Phyllis and I felt almost comfortable in seeing my vision of expectation. This figure in blue pulled at my heart strings in a manner of never before and never since.

Phyllis was a portly, middle aged Lady, wearing a badly fitting floral frock, shiny tights and very large, mid heeled court shoes.
The eyeshadow was very, very, blue.

I remember thinking that the delightful Phyllis, sadly, had no help with her fashion and in looking around the room, I realised that besides Dierdre and myself, there was only one other natural born woman at the event.

The other Lady who was accompanied by her Wife favoured the maiden aunt look and both wore high necked, pastel blouses, beige calf length A line skirts and almost flat, pale, court shoes. Surprisingly, Anastasia's makeup, though neutral, was a little gaudy. I put this down to her Wife's disinterest in her own makeup.

I had made it clear that I would be unable to hold hands or physically behave as a Wife whilst Zabina was with me. Anastasia and her Wife were constantly touching and kissing, but I could not stretch to that. Thankfully, my Husband was comfortable with my feelings and simply appreciated the fact that I was there at all.

It was noticeable how these Ladies treated me respectfully, with the attitude of a man looking at a real woman. The fact that I am a woman and they were biological men was, genuinely, somewhat of a relief, although I still didn't see it as quite "normal."

One person didn't fit into the natural order of the evening. The Lady in the style of the Ladyboy seemed to have little in common with the others. She looked perfect. And she could pass. But in being perfect, she had lost her last trace of obvious, outward maleness.

Sub-genders of cross-dressing, as we know, do not always mix well.
And the others did not want to be perfect.
They just wanted to belong.

The evening was a mixture of magical surprises and amazingly, mostly normal conversation. I had expected talk of makeup and clothes, like silly teenage girls laughing together, but it was nothing like that at all.

A glass of wine was placed in my hand and I sat next to my Husband, something I had not expected to readily accept. As I predicted, I was not ready to snuggle up on the sofa, but we were able to sit together, in company and talk to the others.

However, I really enjoyed talking to the others, who of course, were not involved directly in my life. I felt reassured that I was still sane.

After a while, the conversations did turn towards why people had attended. A few life stories emerged, including Anastasia, whose Wife was her second. This was unusual for the time, but the tale of how they met and fell in love followed. Which explained why they were still so close – Anastasia was never a secret to her Wife.

It was less easy for others, as stories emerged in brief but poignant bursts. Stories of love, lies and loss, interwoven with hope, need and sadness.

Phyllis did not offer her story, but I suspect it was a lonely one.

Again, my heart went out to the room. Normal people, with an agonising secret which could rarely be shared. The pain we witnessed was all too familiar. My own feelings and issues bonded through association and for that, I shall be forever grateful.

It did not, of course, solve my own problems, but I no longer felt alone. This was not a solitary confinement, or something which happened only to me and my Husband. It did, in fact, seem that the cross-dressing scenario is certainly not a rarity, just a hidden one.

I felt so privileged to have been in that room.

To my amazement, my Husband had indeed been correct. These hybrid pseudo-ladies had the strange desire to dress and look like a woman but could in no way be confused with natural born women.

And they behaved like men.
Well, they were, after all, biological men.

The journey home was a light-hearted one. We were full of ourselves, of life, buoyant in our mood and well, absurdly proud of ourselves. We had done it; survived.

My Husband had achieved his ambition to take Zabina out and had done so with the flying colours of dignity, if perhaps lacking a little in grace. We laughed about the stilettos, how it wasn't quite so easy to glide smoothly down a sweeping flight of strange stairs, especially when trying to keep up with the speed and confidence of a gangster's moll.

We congratulated ourselves on our togetherness, the bravado of us both and simply for our courage to be there. It was a milestone.

There was much talk about the company, the bizarre and exotic people we had met; we compared notes about the things we had observed.

Mostly, we agreed on the good, the bad and even the plain ugly. There was so much emotion, empathy and obviously we discussed the characters, from drab to flamboyant, likeable to out of place.

We were introduced to them all and without exception they were lovely people. The majority had normal lives and were struggling to cope with their dual personalities. Just like Zabina.

My Husband had found Anastasia and her Wife "weird, even I find them strange, I wouldn't expect you to be all over me when I was dressed like that." I lightened the moment by adding that to be honest, I wouldn't have dressed like Anastasia's Wife, either.

Neither of us found it easy to connect with the Ladyboy Lady. Her confidence was frightening and we felt that she actually did not mix comfortably with our own sub-genre of cross-dressers, the "normal" men. I was shocked at my sudden level of subtle understanding.

Back home, we drank the inevitable bottle of wine. If I had a bottle of champagne, I would have opened it. We talked and relived, relived and analysed. But I didn't want that night to end. I did not want to go to bed and wake as my Husband's Wife on a normal day.

I knew that for now, I would stay.
But my physical revulsion to Zabina's touch remained unchanged.

Boundaries of Revelation

There is not much more to tell. The never ending question of what comes next becomes less exciting.

We had done it all, faced the demons, the fears.
Faced the Nemesis.

We lived on and our daily lives continued, with Zabina's lair woven into our outward normality. Zabina was our normal, as she had always been, ever since the moment we were introduced.

We never returned to Dierdre's house. As often happens when people get old, Dierdre became ill. There was much hope for recovery, but as time passed, there was no recovery. The social evenings had stopped and My Husband never found a replacement. I often thought of Phyllis with affection and hoped she was well.

I developed an aura, a persona which attracted a certain type of Lady into my company, as if they instinctively knew they would be safe within my circle. I never let on about my past, but my memory of Phillis always ensured that I looked them in the eye and spoke kindly to the people inside. Just seeing the joy of that passing moment of true acceptance was priceless. I hope it helped.

We retired, with time to enjoy life. Spending every moment together sometimes became a strain, but we were better equipped for this than most newly retired couples.

I took to visiting friends and family, taking days out when I wanted, occasionally treating myself to a holiday in a rented mobile home. But not in a field, the days of lone homes in a corner had long been replaced by modern leisure parks.

Anyway, it was wise not to get too nostalgic about the past.

These absences gave my Husband the chance to be at home with Zabina, as and when he chose. He developed an extensive wardrobe, all of his own. This was the alternative to keeping my own clothes in the car, which was far too small for the purpose.

Although, through habit, I always kept my vintage stilettos locked away in a suitcase, with a little silver key.

The Mirror Reprise

So, who do you see
Looking back from the mirror?
    Is She your friend
    Or your ultimate foe?

        Is She the Nemesis
        Trying to destroy you?
            Or is she your guide on
            A path which you know?

Many have tried
But there's no explanation
    No-one prepares you
    For one massive shock

        You know the Lady
        A Lady so beautiful
            Others will see
            Just a man in a frock

What Happened To Brianna?

I will leave the final chapter of my fate to your own imagination.

Did my Husband and I continue or was I whisked away by a new tide of life?

I do not reveal the ending, because if this is also your story, I will not influence your own conclusion. You must choose your own path.

What I will tell you, is that without Zabina, my life would have been less colourful, less fulfilling.

It would have been much more ordinary.

Without Zabina, I would not have followed my heart and lived two lives. I would not be the woman that I am.

And without Zabina, my Husband may well have left to pursue an affair with someone else, a woman who did not live in a suitcase.

Finally, without Zabina's secrets, the conflict, the bond which we shared from youth to retirement, I doubt that I would have stayed at all. There is, indeed, much loyalty in shared secrets.

Sometimes, in the face of adversity, if we are brave enough to look directly at our Nemesis, we can see human nature at its best.

And sometimes, it is enough.

Zabina, my Nemesis

The Man In My Shoes
My Cross-dressing Husband

www.ingramcontent.com/pod-product-compliance
Lightning Source LLC
Chambersburg PA
CBHW062121040426
42336CB00041B/2179